PREDICTING
EARTHQUAKES

PREDICTING EARTHQUAKES

BY GREGORY VOGT

Franklin Watts ▪ *1989*
New York ▪ *London* ▪ *Toronto* ▪ *Sydney*

Library of Congress Cataloging-in-Publication Data

Vogt, Gregory.
Predicting earthquakes / by Gregory Vogt.
p.   cm. —
Bibliography: p.
Includes index.
Summary: Describes the devastating effects of earthquakes and how
they are predicted, located, and measured.
ISBN 0-531-10788-4
1. Earthquake prediction—Juvenile literature.   [1. Earthquake
prediction.   2. Earthquakes.]   I. Title.
QE538.8.v63   1989
551.2'2—dc20   89-8996 CIP AC

*This book is dedicated with
affection and respect to
Reverend Malcom P. Brunner
whose booming church voice
has been known to set off
more than a few earthquakes.*

Diagrams by: Vantage Art

CONTENTS

Chapter One
"A Chasm Opened beneath Me"
▪ 11 ▪

Chapter Two
The Quaking Earth
▪ 23 ▪

Chapter Three
Measuring the Earthquake's Pulse
▪ 43 ▪

Chapter Four
A Moving Jigsaw Puzzle
▪ 62 ▪

Chapter Five
Forecasting
Earthquakes and
Controlling
Their Effects
▪ 73 ▪

Glossary
▪ 101 ▪

For Further Reading
▪ 105 ▪

Index
▪ 107 ▪

PREDICTING

EARTHQUAKES

PREDICTING

ONE

"A CHASM OPENED BENEATH ME"

Late in the afternoon on March 27, 1964, Robert B. Atwood was relaxing in his home located in the elegant Turnagain Heights subdivision overlooking Anchorage, Alaska, from the southwest. Built on a bluff of clay, sand, and gravel, the subdivision featured some of the city's finest homes. At 5:36 P.M., Atwood felt his house shake, not an uncommon experience for a region prone to earthquakes, and he ran outside. Much later, he reported on what had happened in the moments that followed—now known as the "Good Friday Earthquake."

I had just started to practice playing the trumpet when the earthquake occurred. In a few short moments it was obvious that this earthquake was no minor one: the chandelier made from a ship's wheel

■ 11 ■

swayed too much. Things were falling that had never fallen before. I headed for the door. At the door I saw walls weaving. On the driveway I turned and watched my house squirm and groan. Tall trees were falling in our yard. I moved to a spot where I thought it would be safe, but, as I moved, I saw cracks appear in the earth. Pieces of ground in jigsaw-puzzle shapes moved up and down, tilted at all angles. I tried to move away, but more appeared in every direction. I noticed that my house was moving away from me, fast. As I started to climb the fence to my neighbor's yard, the fence disappeared. Trees were falling in crazy patterns. Deep chasms opened up. Table-top pieces of earth moved upward, standing like toadstools with great overhangs, some were turned at crazy angles. A chasm opened beneath me. I tumbled down. I was quickly on the verge of being buried. I ducked pieces of trees, fence posts, mailboxes, and other odds and ends. Then my neighbor's house collapsed and slid into the chasm. For a time it threatened to come down on top of me, but the earth was still moving, and the chasm opened to receive the house.

Like most other residents of the Turnagain Heights subdivision, Atwood was lucky. Others were not. Twelve-year-old Perry Mead was home babysitting his two younger brothers and sister at the time. Acting quickly, Perry got them all outside and, dragging them along, reached what he thought was safe ground. Suddenly, a crevasse opened beneath Perry and his two-year-old brother Merrel. Perry's other brother and sister could do nothing as Perry and Merrel plummeted out of sight. Neither was ever found.

All over the Anchorage area there were similar stories of people and buildings shaken to the ground

*Damage caused by the Alaskan
earthquake of March 1964*

in the great earthquake. At first, the quake was felt as a gentle rocking of the ground, much like the rocking of a boat at anchor. Inside houses, plates on shelves began to rattle. Soon the vibrations increased and whole buildings began to shake. The ground itself heaved in giant waves like the ripples in a pond when a large stone is tossed in the water. Next, whole blocks of houses began sliding about, and the pavement opened in fissures as wide as 30 feet (9 m).

In one part of town, a new and fortunately still unoccupied apartment building collapsed in a heap of rubble. A fissure beneath the Government Hill Elementary School opened, splitting apart the school so that part of the building dropped into the crevasse. Fortunately, no one was inside the school at the time. In many areas of the city and the surrounding region, all buildings taller than one story were leveled to the ground. The tall concrete air-traffic-control tower at the Anchorage airport collapsed, killing one person. Railroad cars were tossed about and railroad tracks were twisted like pretzels. Roads and highways stretching for miles and miles were split, twisted, and ripped apart.

As the quake energy vibrations rippled through the surrounding countryside at speeds of nearly 7,200 miles (11,600 seconds) per hour, bluffs of mounded sediments cascaded into the sea setting off huge waves that smashed into the land on the other side of the bay with walls of water 30 feet high. Anchored ships bobbed like corks. Seafloor movements triggered even larger waves, called *tsunamis,* that raced outward. In Valdez, to the south, $11 million worth of property damage was done by a wave that reached the port five hours later and heaped itself up along with the rising tide. The entire mass of water in the Prince William Sound sloshed about. When it ended, 68 fishing craft were missing and 32 people had lost their lives. Tsunami waves continued across the Pacific Ocean, eventually slamming into Hawaii and Japan.

The Good Friday Earthquake was among the largest of all earthquakes in historic time and possibly the largest ever felt in U.S. history. By one estimate, the energy released was equivalent to the simultaneous explosion of 240 million tons of TNT. In its massive release of energy, more than 100,000 square miles of the earth's surface either heaved upward or subsided. Buildings in Seattle, Washington, swayed, and as far away as Cape Canaveral, site of NASA's manned space launches, land was uplifted by 2½ inches. The energy released made the entire planet vibrate for two weeks afterwards. Smaller earthquakes known as *aftershocks* followed the main earthquake. By the end of 18 months, more than 10,000 had been recorded.

In spite of the tremendous energy released by the Good Friday Earthquake and the widespread destruction of property it caused, the death toll was relatively low. About 115 people were killed. Of that number, 82 were just presumed to be dead because their bodies, like those of Perry and Merrel Mead, were never found. The low death toll was partly due to the timing of the event. On that Good Friday the sparse population of the region was widely dispersed, and office buildings, stores, and schools were empty.

THE LISBON EARTHQUAKE

The timing of another earthquake, over 200 years before near Lisbon, Portugal, was not so fortunate. Although accurate instruments to measure earthquakes had not been invented yet, the earthquake that struck Lisbon, Portugal, on November 1, 1755

Engraving of the
Lisbon earthquake of 1755

may have been the strongest ever unleashed in all of historic time. Lisbon was, at that time, the wealthy hub of the Portuguese empire. Portuguese explorers had ranged the oceans of the world and brought back treasures of gold, silks, and art.

Like the 1964 Anchorage earthquake, the 1755 Lisbon earthquake also struck on a holiday—All Saints Day. The quake began, however, at 9:40 A.M. when many of Lisbon's population of 250,000 were in church worshiping. At the onset of the quake, the city began to shudder violently. Tall church spires began "waving like a cornfield in a breeze." In the great cathedral Basilica de Santa Maria, the floor rocked and massive chandeliers began swaying widely. Terrified worshipers ran screaming into the streets and met other worshipers coming out from nearby churches. Uncertain what to do, thousands massed in the narrow squares of the city. They had little time to wonder. A second shock that shook loose ornate stone decorations from church exteriors hit the city. A rain of stones fell on the cowering people below and heaped up rubble onto mass graves.

Many buildings in the city, weakened by the first shock, fell with the second. A survivor reported, "In some places lay coaches, with their masters, horses and riders almost crushed to pieces; here mothers with infants in their arms; there ladies richly dressed, friars, gentlemen, mechanics. Some had their backs or thighs broken; others vast stones on their breasts; some lay almost buried in the rubbish."

In other parts of the city, hundreds rushed to seek refuge on a newly built marble pier by the Tagus River. The first earthquake shock caused the river to recede, but by the time of the second shock, the river returned in a 50-foot (15 m) crest that surged over the pier and into the city. The huddling people were pulled into and drowned in a maelstrom of water, splintering ships, and cargo.

The ordeal of Lisbon was not yet over. The tremors knocked over candles on church altars, igniting tapestries and vestments. In homes, wooden roofs collapsed inward and the wood was ignited by fires in cooking hearths. At first the blazes were small and generally ignored by the dazed citizens. Then the individual fires spread and joined to become a new holocaust. For three days the fire raged, and most of the wooden structures that had survived the quakes were burned to a smoking pile of ash. Most of the treasures of the city were lost. The death toll mounted to 60,000.

EARTHQUAKES—A FACT OF LIFE ON EARTH

Earthquakes are a fact of life on the earth. The "solid" rock beneath our feet is not as solid as we like to think. It is cracked and fissured in a colossal, planetary jigsaw puzzle in which the pieces continually rearrange themselves. No place on the surface of the earth is free from the effects of earthquakes. Even the floor of the sea is alive with earth tremors. Around the world each year more than 1 million earthquakes take place, which means an earthquake hits somewhere every 30 seconds. Most earthquakes are hardly powerful enough to rattle dishes. About 3,000 each year are strong enough to visibly move the earth's surface. A few dozen earthquakes, at most, have the potential to be catastrophic if they strike in the wrong place. One earthquake in China in 1976 killed an estimated three quarters of a million people.

Earthquake statistics are not comforting. Imagine that 7,999 people around the world are reading this book as you are now, 8,000 in all. At some time, an earthquake will end the life of one of you. In other words, the odds that you will be killed by the effects of the trembling earth are 1 in 8,000. The odds are much greater, 1 in 800, that you will be injured during an earthquake. That means 10 of you will sustain earthquake injuries, perhaps by being hit by debris falling from a collapsing building. Still greater are the odds that you will experience an earthquake in your lifetime. Nearly everyone who survives to old age does, and many have felt earthquakes several times during their lives. How many earthquakes you will experience depends upon where you live.

All places on earth are subject to earthquakes, but some places seem to have more than their fair share while others, less. If you live in the Mississippi Valley near St. Louis, Missouri, earthquakes may not be a daily fact of life for you. Earthquakes there are very rare, and your chances of being injured or killed by one are lessened merely by geography. However, you are probably not completely safe because some of the largest earthquakes ever felt in the United States were centered just a short distance away near New Madrid, Missouri. Three earthquakes struck there during the winter of 1811–1812.

Other earthquakes are possible in the future. If you live near Los Angeles, California, you have probably already experienced an earthquake and will feel several more if you continue to live there. At least one of the earthquakes you have felt or will feel will produce serious results. Earthquakes are a frequent occurrence along the western coast of the United States.

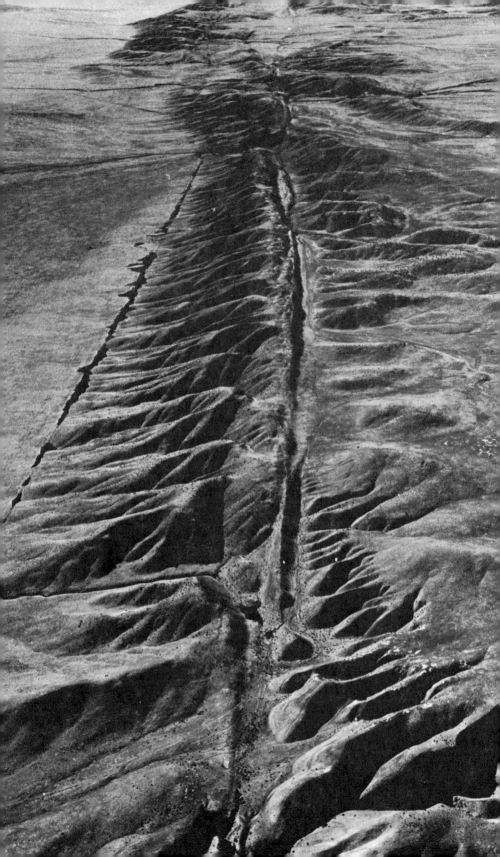

.In the United States more than 70 million people live in regions where the potential hazard from earthquakes is classified as "severe." Another 120 million or so people live in a region classified as "moderate" in earthquake danger. The rest live in places where the danger is "low" and practically never have to worry about earthquakes, provided they never take a trip somewhere else!

If you are present in an area where an earthquake hits, what happens to you depends upon many factors. The most important are how close you are to the source of the earthquake, how powerful the earthquake is, and exactly where you are when the movements of the earth reach you. If you are outside on stable ground and away from objects that can fall on you, the only thing that might happen is that you may be knocked off your feet. If, however, you are standing inside a poorly constructed apartment building, you may find the entire building collapsing around you.

Yet as dangerous as earthquakes are, we owe much to them. The forces that crack and shatter the earth are one result of a major system of crustal movements that move entire continents like large sheets of ice in a flowing river. Like ice sheets, the continents bump and grind and crack together. These giant crustal pieces are called *tectonic plates*. Slowly, over millions of years, majestic mountains are thrust up at the points where these plates collide. The mountains then wear away, producing the soils of

Portion of the San Andreas fault in southern California

some of the great farm regions of the world. Without those forces continuously moving and mounding up the crust of the earth, the earth's land forms would probably have eroded into featureless, swampy plains.

What are the forces that move whole continents? What happens during an earthquake? How are earthquakes measured? Do earthquakes send out warning signs that movement is about to take place? Can earthquakes be forecasted in advance so that human lives can be spared by evacuating people to safety? Can earthquakes be controlled? *Seismologists,* the scientists who study earthquakes, have learned much about earthquakes, but much is yet to be learned.

PREDICTING

TWO

THE QUAKING EARTH

Earthquakes are in some ways the most fearsome natural force on earth. Unlike other disasters such as volcanoes, hurricanes, and tornadoes, there is no escaping an earthquake. Everything moves at once. With other natural forces of destruction there is usually some warning before the disaster strikes. A volcano may issue large columns of black smoke and steam weeks before the big eruption begins. A prudent person simply leaves the area to go to safety. Violent storms are preceded by a buildup of dark clouds and quick changes in the wind. A prudent person seeks a sturdy shelter. What does one do about an earthquake, in which tens of thousands of square miles may be in motion, except "ride it out"?

An earthquake may strike anywhere and usually does so without any easily noticeable warnings. The day of a major earthquake begins like any other. The peace is suddenly shattered with a trembling like the arrival of a heavily loaded freight train. Soon the ground begins heaving violently, as ocean water does during a storm, throwing people to the ground and making it nearly impossible to get up. Waves may travel across solid pavement. Buildings will sway and twist and come tumbling down. There is a rumbling sound like the continuous roar of distant cannon. Long cracks will snake across the countryside. Cliffs may form along the cracks as one side drops or raises in relation to the other.

Other cracks may open wide to form gaping crevasses. Next may come giant waves of water that will streak across oceans to smash distant shores. Finally, small fires may break out from spilled fireplace hearths and ruptured natural gas lines ignited by sparks that combine into fire storms to sweep across the landscape, completing the destruction begun by the earth movements. Except for the fires and the ocean-traveling waves, the calamity may end in just seconds—a few minutes at the most.

EARLY THEORIES

Just what is an earthquake? There have been many explanations, including the fanciful beliefs, grounded in religion and mythology, of ancient peoples. Primitive people were unaware that the earth is round. To them, the land was level and extended in all directions as far as the eye could see. In Hindu mythology, the earth was a platform that rested on the back of eight great elephants. When one of the elephants grew weary, it lowered and shook its head, causing the ground above to tremble.

The Greeks blamed earthquakes on Poseidon, god of the sea. The Hebrews indirectly attributed earthquakes to the wrath of God. The Biblical story of God's destruction of the wicked cities of Sodom and Gomorrah is believed, in one theory, to have been based on a terrible earthquake that struck the region. During the quake, cooking fires ignited natural gas that was released from the soil and the rocky bitumen building materials used to construct the cities. Bitumen has a high petroleum content and will burn furiously once ignited. The two cities disappeared in a conflagration that left only ashes behind.

Early "scientific" explanations of earthquakes were offered by Babylonian astronomers who believed an alignment of the sun and stars triggered ground-shaking. The Greek philosopher Aristotle thought earthquakes took place when external winds blew through underground caves and built up pressure that only could be relieved by shaking the earth. Like the Babylonians, Aristotle had no proof for his explanation. In later years, Benjamin Franklin speculated that electricity might be responsible for earthquakes. One English scientist believed earthquakes were caused by steam pressure created when underground water made contact with the earth's internal fires.

With centuries of scientific investigation on earthquakes now behind us, we know the real origin of earthquakes. They are caused by a break or giant crack in the solid rock of the earth that moves. The crack is called a *fault,* and during the earthquake both sides of the fault move in relation to each other. This movement is caused by the tremendous pressures and tensions that build up within the not-so-solid earth.

The amount of movement may be very small, or the two sides may suddenly shift perhaps as much as 100 feet (30 m) in relation to each other. It is this movement that creates the intense vibrations felt on the surface of the earth as an earthquake.

THE FAULTED EARTH

Geologists know about faults in the solid rock of the earth because old faults are found nearly everywhere where rock is exposed on the surface. By careful observation and measurement, geologists, acting like detectives, can tell how much a fault moved, which part went up and which part went down, what direction the fault moved, and when it moved—even though the movement producing an earthquake may have taken place hundreds of millions of years ago.

Three general kinds of faults have been identified: *normal, reverse,* and *strike-slip* (Figure 1). A fault is categorized according to its angle and the direction of the movement of the rock around it. Geologists determine the angle and movement of a fault by looking at the rock the fault cuts across. Most of the rock at the earth's surface is sedimentary. This means that the rock was created from sand or mud or gravel or some combination of different materials that was laid down at the bottom of an ancient ocean. The rock hardened in horizontal layers. Much later, pressures or tensions in the region will trigger earthquakes that will crack or fault the rock causing the two sides of the fault to move. The surface or face of the fault, as it extends through the rock, is called the *fault plane,* and it almost always cuts across the rock at some angle other than parallel to the layers of the rock.

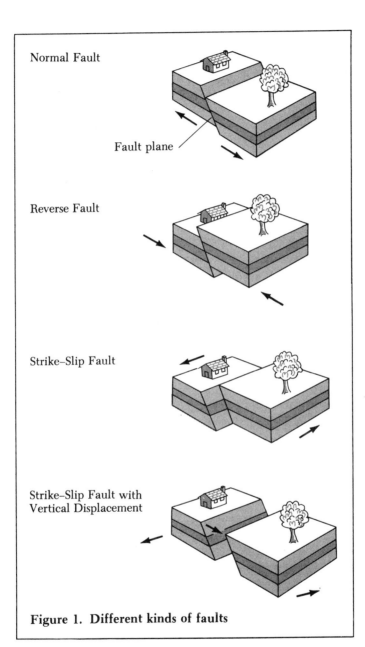

Normal Fault

Fault plane

Reverse Fault

Strike–Slip Fault

Strike–Slip Fault with
Vertical Displacement

Figure 1. Different kinds of faults

During the earthquake movement of the rock along the fault plane, one side moves up, down, or sideways in relation to the other. The uniform horizontal beds of the sedimentary rock are now offset. One side is higher than the other or has moved some distance away horizontally. How far the beds are offset from each other tells how much movement took place even if that movement took place millions of years ago.

A fault consists of three main parts. The fault plane is the crack itself. When viewed just from its edge, the fault plane looks like a line and is called, simply, the *fault line*. The rocks on each side of the fault have names given by miners who found faults excellent places to mine for minerals. Stretching deep into the earth, faults provide easy routes for hot solutions of minerals to work their way toward the surface. When the solutions cool, minerals like gold, copper, and silver are deposited as veins in the fault. Miners blast and chip the rock along the fault to remove the mineral ore. Because of the inclination of the fault plane, the miners usually find themselves walking on the rock of one side of the fault with the rock of the other side of the fault hanging over their heads. This arrangement led to the terms *footwall* and *hanging wall*. The footwall side of the fault slopes under the hanging-wall side (Figure 2).

By using the terms fault line, footwall, and hanging wall, it is now possible to define the three general kinds of faults mentioned earlier. A normal fault results when tensions in the earth try to pull rock apart. What happens instead is that the hanging-wall side of the fault line moves downward, and the footwall moves upward. A normal fault also occurs when just the footwall moves upward and the hanging

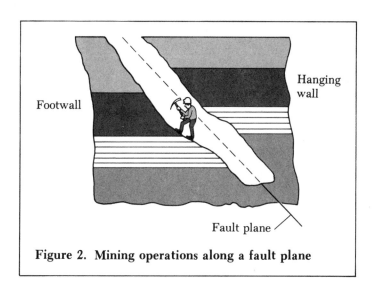

Figure 2. Mining operations along a fault plane

wall remains stationary, or the hanging wall may just drop and the footwall remain stationary. In the end, the movement of the two sides of the normal fault have actually stretched the earth's surface farther apart. This can be seen because trees or buildings on opposite sides of the fault line are actually farther apart after the earthquake that caused the fault than before.

Movement of the hanging wall and footwall in a reverse fault is the reverse of that in a normal fault. The reverse fault is produced by pressure within the earth trying to push the rock together. Instead of coming together, the rock faults and the hanging wall move upward in relation to the footwall. As in the normal fault, one or the other wall may move or they both may move to produce the effect. With reverse faults, surface features on opposite sides of the fault line get closer together.

The strike-slip fault is one in which the hanging wall and footwall move in opposite directions to each other, with both sides maintaining the same height. The name of this kind of fault comes from the word *strike*. A strike is an imaginary horizontal line on the surface of layers of rock. Many sedimentary rocks do not lie perfectly horizontal because pressures within the earth have caused them to tilt. For mapping purposes, geologists calculate the direction of tilt of these rocks by measuring where a horizontal line would lie on their surfaces. This is the strike, and the tilt or dip of the rock's surface is measured from it. In a strike-slip fault the two sides move or slide past each other in directions parallel to the strike. To understand what this might look like, imagine placing two bricks on a table and sliding them in opposite directions past each other. Strike-slip faults can be caused by compressional forces or by tensional forces in the crust of the earth.

In practice, many faults are a combination of normal and strike-slip or reverse and strike-slip. In other words, while the hanging wall and footwall are moving vertically past each other, they may also be moving in a direction parallel to the fault. The result is an angular displacement.

The surface effects of faulting within the earth are many. Compressional forces pushing rock together to produce reverse faults can thrust up large blocks of rock to form mountain chains. The buildup will take place over millions of years rather than all at once. In time, the effects of thousands of earthquake-producing fault movements add up to great heights. Tensional forces can cause large blocks of land to subside to form wide valleys. A series of three huge earthquakes near New Madrid, Missouri in the winter of 1811–12 turned thousands of acres of prairie into swamplands. During those earthquakes, fields and riverbanks were jumbled with a maze of furrows and crevasses, some so wide horses could not jump across. One lake bed was raised and drained to become a dry field while in another area a new lake formed. Islands disappeared from the Mississippi River.

Large masses of rocks moving past one another will grind the rock at the fault line, softening it to make it more susceptible to wearing away. In the end, the fault line may be marked with a long and deep V-shaped *rift* valley.

Earthquakes also create secondary effects such as landslides of rock and soil that fall from steep-walled valleys. An earthquake in 1959 that struck the Yellowstone National Park region tore loose the face of a Montana mountain alongside the Madison River. The rock slide dammed the river, creating Earthquake Lake, and buried 28 summer campers who were asleep in their tents.

ELASTIC ROCKS

It may seem strange, but rocks are elastic. In other words, rocks can bend under pressure. The pressure has to be exerted for a very long time, and it cannot be so great as to cause the rock to crack. If the pressure is removed, the rocks will eventually unbend themselves. However, if the pressure lasts long enough, the bends will become permanent even if the pressure is taken away. Geologists call these bends *folds*. Many of the great mountains of the world are laced with folded rock. On the other hand, if the pressure is exerted too rapidly, the rock will break or fault, producing an earthquake. The rocks on the opposite

"Quake Lake" in Yellowstone National Park, Montana. The lake was created by an avalanche of rock, dirt, and trees that dammed a river.

sides of the fault line suddenly jump relative to each other and realign themselves in new positions. The process is similar to bending a strip of wood. Eventually the bending force is greater than the strength of the wood, and the wood snaps. The two ends return to their original shape but are now separated by a fault.

Within seconds of the break, the main shock of the rock movement rumbles the earth's surface above. However, additional rumblings or *aftershocks* of a lesser force may follow for hours, days, or months afterward. Some of these aftershocks are caused by the elastic nature of the rock. The rock surrounding the fault plane simply vibrates for a time. Other aftershocks come from adjustments made by the rock in the surrounding countryside. A strong earthquake may shatter surrounding rock in many places, and for months afterward it will settle and in doing so send out small tremors.

After an earthquake occurs along a fault, the pressure that produced the fault and earthquake may continue and build up again. Friction between the rocks on both sides of the fault line will lock the fault sides together temporarily. Such a condition is called a *locked fault*. The rock grains try to deform and dissipate the energy, but there is insufficient time for this to happen. They bend temporarily while waiting to spring back to their old shapes. When the pressure on the sides of the fault exceeds the force of friction holding them together, the fault jumps again to readjust itself and produces another earthquake. This effect can be understood by wrapping two blocks of wood with sandpaper. Press the blocks together and then try to slide them opposite to each other. At first the blocks act like a solid piece of wood, but when the sideways pressure is great enough, the two blocks suddenly slide apart.

WAVES IN THE EARTH

The moment the earth faults or an old locked fault unlocks, months or years of accumulated pressure is suddenly released. The underground point where that release begins is the earthquake's *focus*. The released energy moves outward from the focus and along the length of the fault plane, perhaps a few yards in very small earthquakes to hundreds of miles in very large ones. The depth of the focus beneath the surface of the earth ranges from less than 43 miles (70 km) for shallow focus, to between 43 and 186 miles (70 and 300 km) for intermediate focus, and between 186 and 435 miles (300 and 700 km) for deep focus earthquakes.

Much of the energy released by earthquake movement is dissipated by the shattering and fracturing of surrounding rocks and by being converted into heat through friction or rubbing of the fault plane as movement takes place. A small part of the energy radiates out in all directions as *seismic waves*. The waves travel through the earth something like the ripples on a pond when a stone is tossed in. Earthquake waves, however, travel in three dimensions and move as rapidly expanding spheres. Perhaps a better example of what is taking place would be to imagine several round balloons, one inside the other, all being inflated at the same time. Each balloon represents a growing spherical seismic wave expanding out throughout the earth's interior. When the waves strike the surface of the earth they create the heaving motion we feel during an earthquake. The waves first strike the surface at a point directly above the focus.

That point on the earth's surface is called the *epicenter*, and it is the place where the damage from the earthquake is usually the greatest.

It is difficult to imagine the solid earth being able to carry wave motion, but in fact it does so very efficiently. Several kinds of waves are created by an earthquake, and they fall into two general categories. Waves that travel through the body of the earth are called *body waves*, and those that travel along the surface are called *surface waves*. Body waves come in two kinds—P- and S-waves. Surface waves also come in two kinds—Rayleigh and Love waves.

The fastest-moving body wave is called the *P-wave* (Figure 3). ("P" stands for primary). P-waves are like sound waves. They begin with a compression or a pushing motion, like that caused by a hammer tapping the end of a tabletop. The particles feeling the compression first move slightly and collide with the particles next to them, passing on the energy to the next particles and so on. Immediately upon passing on the wave energy, each particle returns to its original position. Because of this immediate return, P-waves are also called "push-pull" waves. P-waves travel through the rock at a velocity of about 4.8 miles (8 km) per second or 16,200 miles (26,000 km) per hour. At that rate, an observer 100 miles (160 km) away from the earthquake's focus will feel the earthquake just 20 seconds after it strikes.

At the same time the P-wave is produced at the earthquake's focus, an S-wave is also created ("S" stands for secondary). *S-waves* can be thought of as shaking or shear waves (Figure 4). The S-wave travels through the earth very much like the wave produced in a length of rope that is tied at one end and shaken from side to side at the other. The S-wave travels

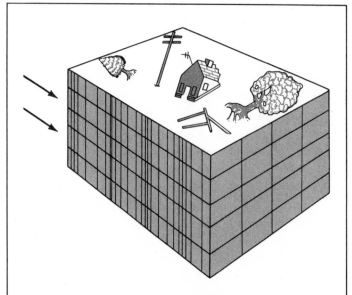

Figure 3. P-waves are caused by earthquake energy transmitted from left to right by compression of the rock (also called push–pull waves).

much more slowly than a P-wave. At 2.75 miles (4.5 km) per second or about 10,000 miles (16,100 km) per hour, S-waves will take 36 seconds to reach an observer 100 miles away. The difference between the arrival times of the two waves provides seismologists with a valuable tool for determining location of the earthquake's focal points deep below the earth's surface.

Surface waves also come in two varieties. They are created when body waves from the earthquake reach the earth's surface. They vibrate more slowly than body waves but are especially persistent and have been known to circle the earth several times

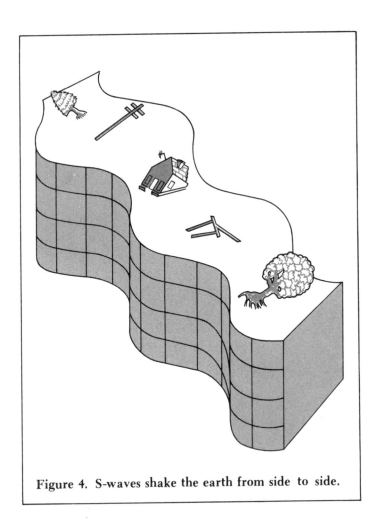

Figure 4. S-waves shake the earth from side to side.

before dissipating. Scientists mathematically predicted the existence of surface waves before actually measuring them. The *Love wave*, named for British mathematician A. E. H. Love, is similar to an S-wave in that it shakes from side to side (Figure 5). However, Love

Figure 5. Love waves, like S-waves, shake the earth from side to side but are confined to the surface of the earth.

waves are confined to the surface of the earth. The shaking motion quickly diminishes with depth. The Love wave is especially destructive to surface structures, literally shaking buildings until they crack and tumble down. Love waves travel at a velocity of just under 2 miles (3.2 km) per second, or 7,200 miles (11,600 km) per hour.

The other surface wave, the *Rayleigh wave,* (named for the British scientist Lord Rayleigh), acts like an ocean wave (Figure 6). The earth's surface heaves upward in a rolling motion that streaks across the land at a speed of 1.7 miles (2.7 km) per second or 6,120 miles (9,850 km) per hour. Rayleigh waves are not as destructive to buildings as Love waves because their main effect is to raise the land. Buildings are designed to stand up under many times their normal weight, and rising and falling land movements beneath don't affect them as much as land movements shaking them from side to side.

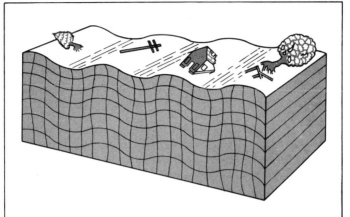

Figure 6. The Rayleigh wave produces a rolling ground motion on the surface.

The actual velocities of body and surface waves vary with the material through which they pass. In general, the denser the material is, the faster the waves will travel through it. You can verify this for yourself if you can locate a long metal fence and have a friend stand at one end of the fence and tap the metal tubing with a hammer. If you place your ear to the other end, you will hear the tapping sound through the metal before the sound travels through the air to reach your other ear. P-waves can travel through any kind of material. The roaring sound like that of an approaching freight train some people hear during earthquakes is the P-wave transmitting through the air. S-waves, on the other, can only travel through solid materials. They do not travel through liquids or gas.

TSUNAMIS

The Alaskan Good Friday Earthquake in 1964 brought a different type of tragedy to the 80 residents of Chenega Island in southwestern Prince William Sound. The trembling of the earth had barely started when the waters of the sound began retreating from the beach. The three daughters of Nicholas Kompkoff were down on the beach, and he ran to them as quickly as he could. Scooping up the two youngest daughters, he ran back up the hill to high ground as his third daughter ran by his side. A great sea wave soon followed and caught the four from behind. The wave smashed 100 feet (30 m) up the hillside. When it sloshed back into the sound, two of Kompkoff's daughters and 21 other villagers were gone forever. Kompkoff himself and one of the daughters he carried were thrown farther up the hill by the wave. When the wave receded, every home in the village, and the church, were gone. Four hours later, more waves struck Crescent City, California, 1,800 miles (2,900 km) from Anchorage. The waves killed 11 more people, and many months were required to repair the damage it did to the buildings surrounding the harbor.

Chenega Island and Crescent City both fell prey to a *tsunami*, an ocean wave triggered by an earthquake. Tsunami is a Japanese word meaning "harbor wave." It is a high-speed wave that can travel across entire oceans to smash distant shores.

Crescent City, California,
before (top) and after (bottom)
the tsunami of March 28, 1964

Most tsunamis are caused by the sudden uplift or dropping of ocean floor in the area of the earthquake. The vertical change in the seafloor transmits a large amount of energy to the water. It is like a shallow water-filled pan in which one end is suddenly moved up or down. The water moves and sloshes off the low end of the pan. The tsunami wave, usually one of several that move across the ocean one after another, travels through the water at speeds of more than 400 miles (645 km) per hour.

In deep ocean water, tsunamis are barely noticeable. The distance between the crest (top) of one tsunami and the crest of the next one that follows may be hundreds of miles. A ship in deep water will rise only a few feet as the crest passes, barely enough to disturb its passengers. In shallow water, however, the huge wave energy begins to mound up. The wave crest climbs perhaps 100 feet (30 m) high as the bottom of the wave drags the seafloor bottom slowing its forward speed. The crest slows as well, but not as much as the base, and soon crashes over itself onto the shore. The giant wave obliterates nearly everything in its path.

PREDICTING

THREE

MEASURING THE EARTHQUAKE'S PULSE

As a doctor measures a patient's pulse to gain information about the patient's condition, seismologists measure the earthquake pulse of the earth to learn about the nature of earthquakes and the interior of the earth itself. The seismic waves generated by an earthquake can be traced backward to their source, the focus of the earthquake. The waves tell the amount of energy released by the earthquake. Indirectly, the waves give vital clues to the interior structure of the earth, a place where no scientist has ever been or is likely to go.

EARLY SEISMOMETERS

Taking the earthquake pulse can be tricky because when the seismic waves of a powerful quake reach the observer, everything begins moving at once. For example, how can an observer measure the movement of a building during an earthquake if the land the observer is standing on is moving too? We must use a stable reference point that does not move so that everything else can be measured against it. Long ago, Chinese scholars discovered a stable reference point for measuring earthquakes—*inertia*. Inertia is a property all matter has that causes it to resist changes in motion. It is best seen with a simple experiment. Tie a cord around a heavy weight such as a book. Suspend the weight so that it is just above the floor and hold the other end of the cord with your hand at eye level. This makes the book and cord a *pendulum*. Quickly move your hand from side to side. You will note the book hardly moves at all. The book's inertia resists its movement.

In the second century A.D. Chinese astronomer and mathematician Chang Heng employed inertia when he invented a *seismoscope* for detecting earthquakes. The device was a large vessel surrounded by eight dragons. Each dragon held a bronze ball in its mouth. At the base of the vessel were eight toads with their mouths open. Inside the vessel hung a flexible rod weighted at its upper end. The rod and weight formed an inverted pendulum that would stand very still. If an earthquake struck, the tremors would shake the vessel but leave the pendulum weight undisturbed. During the shaking, one of the bronze balls would be released as it brushed against the stationary pendulum weight. The ball would drop into the toad's mouth below with an alarming clunk to alert Chang Heng that an earthquake had taken place. The particular ball that fell out also provided Heng with a crude idea of the direction from which the earthquake struck.

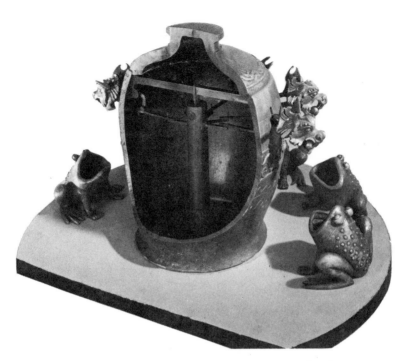

Model of Cheng Heng's seismoscope, the first
earthquake detector (second century A.D.).
Note the pendulum, which remains stationary
during earthquake tremors. The shaking
of the vessel releases the balls.

In later centuries, seismometers took many
forms. One early seismometer consisted of a heavy
pendulum suspended from the ceiling. Connected to
the pendulum was a pointer whose tip dragged in a
tray of fine sand. Whenever an earthquake struck, the
tremors caused the tray to move while the pendulum
remained still. The pointer traced out small furrows in
the sand to record the earthquake's occurrence. A
19th-century seismometer consisted of a shallow dish
filled to the brim with mercury. Earthquake waves
caused the mercury to slosh out of the dish into
smaller collecting dishes at its base.

Early earthquake-measuring devices, such as the 18th-century device that made grooves in sand, caused much confusion for seismologists because the squiggles for different earthquakes would lie on top of each other. Unless someone was there to smooth the sand between earthquakes, the record was a hopeless mess. Later instruments used a pen to make marks on a stationary piece of paper, but these too got confused. To make matters worse, these records did not permit seismologists to examine the nature of the earthquake waves arriving at the instrument. Did the waves change during the earthquake? Were they stronger at the beginning of the earthquake and weaker later, or was it the other way around? The solution to this confusing recording problem was simple—make marks on a moving strip of paper so that the records of different earthquakes would be kept separate. Moving the paper turned the repeated side-to-side motion of the pen into a zigzag line (Figure 7).

MODERN SEISMOGRAPHS

Modern-day *seismographs* (seismometers that show not only that motion has taken place but also create a detailed record of ground movements) still function on the inertia principle of Heng's instrument. They consist of two parts: a seismometer, the heavy weight that remains still as the earth is moving, and some sort of record-keeping device.

Many different arrangements for suspending the seismometer have been tried through the years. One of the best arrangements is to place a heavy weight on the end of a boom that is hinged to an upright post. Thin wires from the top of the post support the weight so that it is free to swing from side to side. Though

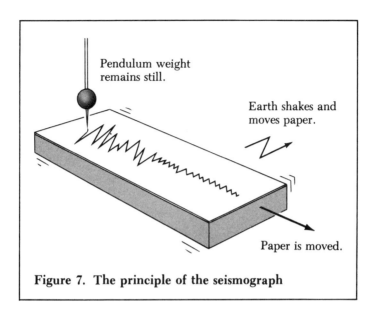

Pendulum weight remains still.

Earth shakes and moves paper.

Paper is moved.

Figure 7. The principle of the seismograph

held differently than the weights in earlier seismic instruments, the weight still serves as a pendulum and its inertia holds it still while the earth and the rest of the seismograph moves underneath it. On the opposite side of the weight from the boom is a pen for marking on paper. The recording device is a rotating drum that has paper wrapped around it. The drum usually rotates completely either once or four times per hour. As it rotates, the drum is also moved slightly to the side so that each time the drum has made one complete circle, the pen mark has moved over a bit and doesn't cross its first marks. Every minute, the needle makes a small tick mark so that the time of any earthquake motions recorded on the drum can be read off to the nearest hour, minute, and second.

One disadvantage to this kind of seismograph is that earthquake movements arriving at the seismograph in a direct line with the boom will not cause the boom to produce a record on the drum. The boom only swings from side to side, not forward and back. A simple solution to the problem is to have two identical seismographs set up at right angles to each other. Regardless of the direction from which the earthquake waves come, at least one seismograph will trace a record on the drum.

Another arrangement for the heavy weight is to suspend it from a thin filament, slightly off center (Figure 8). Whenever the earth shakes, the weight's inertia tries to hold it still. The movement of the seismograph causes the weight to twist around the filament. The recording device for this kind of seismograph may use light-sensitive photographic paper. A narrow light beam bounces off a mirror attached to the weight and onto the rotating drum covered with the light-sensitive paper. The light beam makes the record on the paper. Still another recording method is to use an electromagnetic detector for the movements of the weight. The weight is magnetized, and its movements will generate an electric current in nearby coils of wire. The current is amplified and an electric needle makes the record, or the current is converted into digital form and stored in a computer for later analysis.

The seismographs described so far are only able to record movements of the earth parallel to the ground surface. Earthquake waves also produce heaving vertical to the ground surface. To measure vertical waves, a seismograph similar to the seismograph with the pendulum weight held by a boom is used (Figure 9). A heavy weight is mounted to the end of a boom

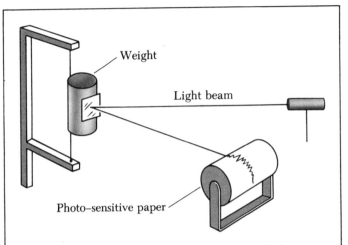

Weight

Light beam

Photo–sensitive paper

Figure 8. A horizontal motion seismograph detects motion from any direction. The weight remains still (because of inertia) as the earth moves.

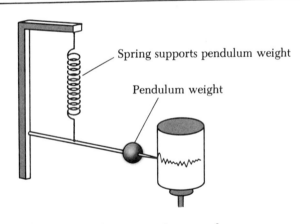

Spring supports pendulum weight

Pendulum weight

Figure 9. Vertical motion seismographs measure heaving of the earth vertical to the ground surface. The weight remains still while the earth moves up and down.

that is attached to a vertical post. Rather than using thin wires to support the weight, a spring is used. During vertical earthquake movements, the spring permits the weight to remain stationary as the rest of the instrument rises up and down.

With the invention of sensitive seismographs, seismologists noted that earth motions could be recorded continuously. There is always a small amount of movement even when no earthquake is taking place. Such movements are called *microseisms*. They are now known to be caused by a number of different things. Heavy traffic, factories, freight trains, mine and quarry explosions, and many other human activities that produce vibrations within the earth can be felt by nearby seismographs. In addition, microseisms can be caused by natural forces such as the great air pressure changes that take place during hurricanes, the gravitational pull of the moon, heavy rainfall, and a kind of pumping action from ocean waves that can be felt at the sea bottom.

HOW EARTHQUAKES
ARE LOCATED

As seismographs began to improve in accuracy, seismologists discovered a way to locate accurately the focus of earthquakes within the earth and their epicenters on the surface. Early attempts at finding the source of earthquake movements were only marginally successful. Seismologists noted that cemeteries give some indication of location by the direction tombstones topple. Tombstones are likely to fall in a direction parallel to the direction the earthquake waves moved in a manner similar to the dropping balls in the Chinese seismoscope described earlier. If a second cemetery in a town widely separated from the first also has toppled stones, a second direction is noted. Seismologists then simply draw two lines on a map representing the directions the tombstones toppled. The lines are extended and their intersection is where the earthquake is likely to have started. The method works reasonably well, but its accuracy is affected by the different kinds of earth materials the waves pass through on their way to the cemeteries. Directions can be changed somewhat, throwing off the location determination. Furthermore, the method doesn't tell how deep the earthquake fault is within the earth.

A much better technique employs mathematics. Earlier, we learned that earthquakes generate two kinds of body waves—P- and S-waves. Furthermore, we learned that these waves travel at different speeds. P-waves travel approximately 4.8 miles (8 km) per second and S-waves approximately 2.75 miles (4.5 km) per second. Because of their different velocities, P- and S-waves arrive at seismographs at different times. The zigzag record shows first the arrival of the faster P-wave and then the arrival of the slower S-wave (Figure 10). This arrival-time difference provides seismologists with a simple way to calculate how far away the earthquake's focus is.

Imagine an earthquake focus exactly 1 mile (1.61 km) from a seismograph. At 4.8 miles per second, the P-wave takes 0.22 seconds to arrive at the seismograph. More importantly, the S-wave takes 0.3636 seconds to travel the same distance. The difference between the arrival times of the two waves, as measured from the seismic record, is

$$0.3636 - 0.2083 = 0.1553 \text{ seconds.}$$

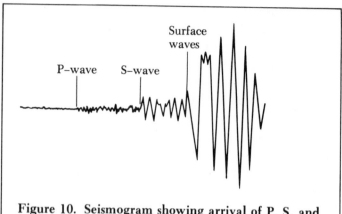

Figure 10. Seismogram showing arrival of P, S, and surface waves.

In other words, for every mile the two waves travel, the S-wave lags behind the P-wave by 0.1553 seconds. If the earthquake focus is 2 miles (3.22 km) away, the difference in arrival times is

$$2 \times 0.1553 = 0.3106 \text{ seconds.}$$

Imagine an earthquake 200 miles (320.2 km) away from the seismograph. The difference in arrival times between the two waves is

$$200 \times 0.1553 = 31.06$$

Now imagine a third earthquake at some unknown distance from the seismograph. First the P-wave arrives and the seismologist measures from the zigzag record when the wave arrived. The seismologist also measures the arrival time of the S-wave (Figure 11).

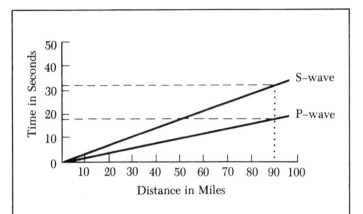

Figure 11. P-and S-waves produced by an earthquake that struck 90 miles (145 km) away. The amount of time it took for the P-wave to arrive at the seismograph can be read from the vertical axis (follow the dashed line). The P-wave arrived in 19 seconds, the S-wave took 33 seconds.

In this case the difference between the waves' arrival times is 62.12 seconds. How far away is the earthquake? The answer is calculated as follows:

$$62.12 \div 0.1553 = 400 \text{ miles away}$$

So far, our method for determining earthquake locations only tells us how far away the earthquake is from the seismograph. We don't know its direction. For that, we need at least two additional seismographs in other locations. The body waves coming from the unknown earthquake arrives at each seismograph at different times. At each location, the seismologist

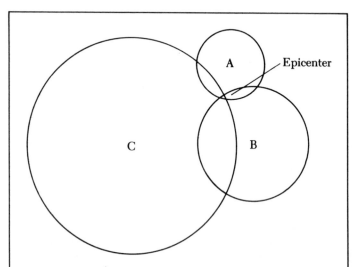

Figure 12. Circles drawn around three seismograph stations will locate the earthquake epicenter. The length of the radii of the circles are determined by the difference in arrival time between P and S waves. Drawing the circles as spheres would locate the focus.

calculates how far away the earthquake is. In our example the earthquake is determined to be 400 miles away from seismograph A, 650 miles from B, and 1,225 miles from C. Its location is determined as follows (Figure 12):

- Seismologists at each station get in touch with each other and compare information. A map of the region that has the exact locations of each seismograph plotted is used.

- A drawing compass is set to a radius of 400 miles according to the map scale, and a circle is drawn around seismograph A.

- A circle with a radius of 650 miles is drawn around B, and a circle with a radius of 1,225 miles is drawn around C. There is only one place where the three circles intersect—the location of the earthquake.

Notice from the figure that the three circles do not intersect exactly. This is because the focus of the earthquake is not located at the earth's surface but at some distance beneath it. If the circles could be drawn as spheres into a three-dimensional earth map, the circles would intersect.

As with most things in life, things are not quite as easy as they first sound. The location technique just presented is confused somewhat by the fact that the velocities of P- and S-waves can vary depending upon the materials they travel through. The distance measurement from one or more of the three seismographs can be off by many tens of miles and this will give a false location for the earthquake. To help solve this problem, seismic records from many seismographs are compared and averaged together so that errors cancel out. This results in a reasonably accurate determination of the earthquake's focus.

Many of the world's seismographs are now linked together in the world wide Standardized Seismograph Network. In the United States, a computerized National Earthquake Information Center (NEIC), located in Colorado, receives data from this network and other sources of seismic data and uses it to

*A geophysicist at the U.S. Geological
Survey's National Earthquake Information
Service in Golden, Colorado, checks
seismographs from around the world.*

Richter noticed that the size or amplitude of the zigzags on a seismograph record varied with the amount of energy the earthquake released. Simply put, big earthquakes produced large zigzags on the seismogram and little earthquakes produced small zigzags. Of course, earthquakes very far away produced small zigzags, but when Richter compensated for the great distance, the zigzag still indicated the power of the earthquake.

Richter created a scale of earthquake magnitude based on the *amplitude* or distance the needle zigzagged on the seismogram. Very small amplitudes were given a number 1. Very large amplitudes, coming from the largest earthquakes, received a 9. The scale didn't stop at 9, but earthquakes larger than 9 are extremely rare. The Richter scale is a bit unusual in that each step has a greater amplitude than the one below it by a factor of 10. This is called a logarithmic scale. In other words, a 2-magnitude earthquake produces an amplitude 10 times greater than a 1-magnitude earthquake. A 3-magnitude earthquake is 10 times greater than a 2 and so on.

The actual amount of energy released by earthquakes classified by the Richter scale varies by a factor of 31 for each magnitude. A 2-magnitude earthquake is 31 times more powerful than a 1-magnitude earthquake and so on. A 3-magnitude earthquake is 31 times more powerful than a 2-magnitude earthquake and is 961 (31 x 31) times more powerful than a 1-magnitude earthquake. A 9-magnitude earthquake is over 850 billion times more powerful than a 1-magnitude earthquake!

PREDICTING

FOUR

A MOVING JIGSAW PUZZLE

The ability to locate earthquake epicenters has provided seismologists with a powerful tool for forecasting where earthquakes may strike next. A place that has been struck once by an earthquake is likely to be struck again. With that thought in mind, seismologists began plotting earthquake epicenters on a world map. A strange pattern emerged. Although earthquakes can strike anywhere on earth, some areas got far more than their "fair share" of earthquakes. A large percentage of the world's earthquakes were concentrated in a ring that surrounded the Pacific Ocean basin. Furthermore, most of the world's active volcanoes were also located there. Was there a relationship between earthquakes and volcanoes? Many earthquakes in other parts of the world had occurred in interesting patterns.

One line of earthquakes struck with regularity beneath the middle floor of the Atlantic Ocean and paralleled the shoreline shapes of the surrounding continents. Other lines of earthquakes interconnected with the mid-Atlantic earthquakes forming a patchwork of earthquake-prone zones. What did the patterns mean?

CONTINENTS ADRIFT

A strong hypothesis as to what was taking place was made by Alfred Wegener, a German meteorologist, in 1912. Wegener pointed out that the continents looked as though they were pieces of a giant jigsaw puzzle in which the pieces were spread apart. The eastern coast of Africa, for example, could nestle comfortably into the Caribbean Sea. He stated the earth's surface was not static but dynamic. The continents were in constant motion and spread apart from each other in a process he called "continental drift." Wegener's colleagues were quick to sneer at his idea because it could not explain what caused the continents to move. In time, however, scientists from around the world began making discoveries that seemed to support Wegener's belief.

Japanese seismologist Kiyoo Wadati discovered, in the 1920s, that the closer the epicenter of an earthquake was to the Asian continent, the deeper its focus was. American seismologist Victor Hugo Benioff discovered a similar occurrence with earthquakes to the west of South America. Benioff wrote a paper in 1954 that suggested that enormous pieces of the Pacific Ocean floor were being thrust beneath the continents. He called the process *subduction* and said it explained why earthquakes were deeper the closer they were to continental borders. Benioff said the

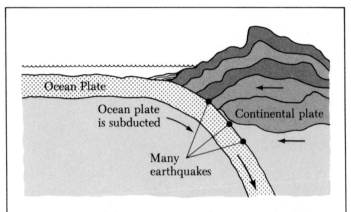

Figure 13. Subduction occurs when one crustal plate thrusts beneath another.

South American continent was ramming into the Pacific Ocean basin, causing the floor of the ocean to be pushed downward into the earth at a steep angle. The subduction of the ocean floor produced a zone of intense earthquake activity that dipped beneath South America (Figure 13). On the other side of the Pacific, Asia was pushing its way into the Pacific basin, causing the ocean floor to subduct beneath it and producing another intense earthquake zone.

As with Wegener, colleagues doubted Benioff's conclusions but were interested in his ideas. They pointed out that Benioff had not explained what caused the continents to move. To investigate this question, Maurice Ewing of Columbia University outfitted a three-masted sailing schooner, the *Vema*, with depth-sounding equipment, seismometers, and other equipment for studying the ocean bottom. For 20 years, starting in 1953, *Vema* crisscrossed the

North and South Atlantic oceans and covered nearly a half million miles (800,000 km). Using explosives, Ewing created powerful seismic waves that bounced off the ocean floor surface and even penetrated the sediments and rock beneath. The reflections enabled Ewing to map the structure of the Atlantic Ocean basin. Among many discoveries was a long, steep mountainlike ridge that cut the Atlantic Ocean down the middle, mirroring the outline of the continental shorelines. It was named the *Mid Atlantic Ridge.*

Rock samples dredged from the ocean floor revealed the ridge to be composed of volcanic basalt rock. Rock samples from the middle of the ridge were younger than rocks found to the east or west. The farther away from the ridge the *Vema* crew sampled rocks, the older the samples were. Even more exciting, a huge crevasse, deeper than the Grand Canyon and 30 miles (48 km) wide, divided the ridge along its middle. At numerous points along the ridge, pieces of the ridge were offset from each other as though giant earthquakes had shifted large portions of the ocean floor. Seismologists quickly discovered that the lines or zones of earthquakes detected previously in the Atlantic Ocean basin matched the location of the ridge. Other ocean ridges were soon discovered in the Pacific and Indian oceans, and these were matched with zones of earthquakes in those areas.

At the time these discoveries were being made, scientists from all over were investigating a new theory of the earth called *plate tectonics.* The theory explained the shapes of the continents and how they came to be where they are. Discoveries about the locations of earthquakes fit neatly into the theory and explained much about why and where earthquakes occur.

According to the theory, the earth's surface is divided up into a dozen or so huge plates or rafts upon which continents are carried. Thermal forces from deep within the earth cause powerful heat-convection currents that propel the plates. Convection currents within the earth are very slow versions of the convection currents in a pot of boiling water that raise the hot water from below to spread out at the surface and then drop down again. The earth's internal heat causes the interior rock of the earth to rise and, when it nears the surface, spread outward.

One place where this spreading takes place is the Mid Atlantic Ridge. Every day, hundreds of thousands of tons of new crust is formed along the ridge by the upthrust of molten material from within the earth. Long ago, the upthrust split open what is now the Atlantic Ocean basin and began pushing it apart. The volcanic rock (basalt) that formed first created a ridge. This was pushed aside by new basalt coming up from the middle, which in turn was eventually pushed aside by the next. The basalt in the center of the ridge was always the youngest and that farthest away to the east and west was the oldest. The pressures of the upthrusting caused and continue to cause numerous earthquakes (Figure 14).

As the ocean floor spread, the plates carrying the continents pushed apart. Europe, Africa, and Asia moved to the east and North and South America to the west—both converging on the Pacific Ocean basin from opposite directions. The continental onslaught forces the thin plates of the Pacific Ocean floor downward as the continental plates ride on top. The ocean plates are subducted downward and eastward at a steep angle along the western margin of South America. Along the eastern margin of Asia, the ocean plates are subducted downward and to the west at a

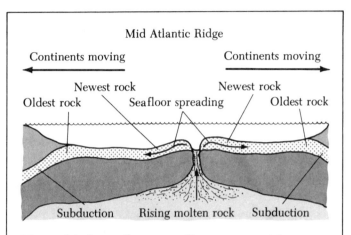

Figure 14. In seafloor spreading, new crust is formed by molten material coming out from within the earth. This pushes the older rock on the surface outward. Geologists believe this is the process by which the Atlantic Ocean has widened and pushed apart the continents.

steep angle. Forcing the ocean plates downward produces massive frictional forces that crumple up leading edges of the continents to produce mountain ridges and causes extensive faulting and earthquake movements. The subducting ocean rocks are heated by the earth's interior. When a deep earthquake fault occurs, pressure on the hot rock is released for a time, causing melting. If the fault interconnects with other faults and reaches up to the surface, the molten material may work its way upward and erupt as a volcano.

The theory of plate tectonics has provided seismologists with the answer to one of their most important questions. What is the source of the energy that causes masses of rock to break and move? Earthquakes are "relief valves" that release the pressure that builds up as the world's plates thrust and drag against each other. Most of the world's earthquakes can be attributed to the pressures built through plate tectonics.

THE EARTH'S INTERIOR

One of the reasons colleagues of Alfred Wegener did not accept his continental drift theory was that Wegener himself believed the continents were made of rock that rammed its way up through the earth's crust. Somehow this rock moved around, but Wegener couldn't come up with a convincing explanation of how it did so. The answer came from the study of earthquake waves.

We know earthquake body waves change velocity depending upon the material they are passing through. The waves released from an earthquake not only travel to the surface but also through the earth's interior. We have already learned that S-waves cannot travel through liquid. Furthermore, liquids greatly slow down the velocity of P-waves. Body waves are also slowed when they pass through warmer rocks. By studying the changes in body wave velocity as the waves pass through the earth's interior, seismologists have pieced together a fairly complete picture of the earth's interior.

From the careful study of seismograms, seismologists have determined that P- and S-waves increase in velocity as they travel deeper within the earth. However, seismologists have noted that S-waves don't increase as fast as they would have anticipated. This slowing of the S-waves takes place at a depth of between 62 and 155 miles (100 and 250 km). Seismologists have labeled this the *low-velocity zone*. The velocity difference indicates the rock there may not be entirely solid. It is more of a plastic or malleable material that can flow slowly. At a depth of about 1,800 miles (2,900 km), S-waves stop entirely, and only P-waves travel through at a lower velocity than before. This would indicate a liquidlike *core* inside the earth. At an even great depth, 3,170 miles (5,100 km), P-waves speed up again. The change indicates an inner core of the earth where the material is no longer liquid and is extremely dense.

Still another earthquake wave measurement of the earth's interior was made by Yugoslavian seismologist Andrija Mohorovičić in 1909. While studying the seismogram of an earthquake, he noticed what appeared to be a second set of P- and S-waves. Mohorovicic reasoned that the second set of waves must be a reflection of the initial waves off some sort of boundary approximately 40 miles (64 km) beneath the surface. The boundary he discovered is now called the Moho Discontinuity. It is the boundary between the crust of the earth and a very thick layer within the earth called the *mantle* (see Figure 15).

These various observations of P- and S-wave characteristics within the earth have enabled scientists to sketch a picture of the structure of the earth's interior. The earth is like a giant egg. The shell of the egg is the rocky crust. Beneath the crust is the plastic mantle or white of the egg. The crust floats on top of the mantle in giant plates, carrying the continents, and convection currents rise up through the mantle to push the plates around, creating many earthquakes and volcanoes in the process. Beneath the mantle is the core (liquid outer core and solid inner core)—the yoke of the egg.

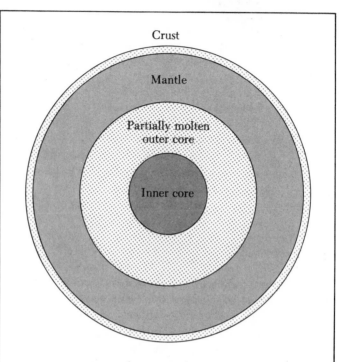

Figure 15. The interior of the earth. Scientists believe the difference in density between the core and the mantle is actually greater than that between the crust and the atmosphere.

NON-PLATE TECTONIC EARTHQUAKES

Understanding the earth's interior has helped explain why thermal currents are able to propel tectonic plates around, triggering many earthquakes. Yet, there are some earthquakes that don't fit the plate-rubbing-against-plate pattern. The earthquakes that struck near New Madrid, Missouri, during the winter of 1811–1812 were examples of such earthquakes. New Madrid is far from the margins of any tectonic plate. Scientists speculate that molten material from the mantle pushed its way up into the bottom of the crust in this area. The rock hardened and is now thought to be a large bump the continent is riding over. Occasionally, friction between the bottom of the crust and the bump is released in giant earthquakes. The bump is called a *pluton*.

Other earthquakes are caused by the movements of molten rock during volcanic eruptions and not directly by moving plates. During those movements of molten rock, the ground is "alive" with tremors. In addition, volcanic mountains that explode cause great earth tremors that are felt by seismographs all around the globe.

MAN-MADE EARTHQUAKES

In 1962, the U.S. Army Rocky Mountain Arsenal near Denver, Colorado, decided to dispose of large amounts of toxic waste by drilling a 5½-inch (14-cm) hole deep into the ground. The area around the well had been free from earthquakes for 80 years. One month after the pumping of water into the ground began, the area was hit by an earthquake. By 1966, the pumping stopped and so did the earthquakes. During those few years, the quiet arsenal area had recorded more than 1,000 earthquakes.

The Rocky Mountain Arsenal experience helped explain what had happened earlier when the Hoover Dam on the Colorado River was finished. The area the dam was built on rarely had earthquakes. As the dam filled up to create Lake Mead behind it, earthquake activity suddenly increased in size and number.

Seismologists pieced together what had happened in both instances. Beneath both areas, old faults were locked by friction. The pressure in the area was not great enough to cause the rocks pressing against the fault planes to move during earthquakes. Water injected into the ground by the arsenal lubricated the fault planes, permitting them to become active and slide, causing numerous small earthquakes. The Hoover Dam created a deep lake behind it where no lake existed before. Water, under pressure from the weight above, seeped deep into the earth beneath the lake bed and lubricated the fault planes present there.

PREDICTING

FIVE

FORECASTING EARTHQUAKES AND CONTROLLING THEIR EFFECTS

The effects of earthquakes can destroy cities and kill people. As the world population continues to expand, it becomes increasingly important to know where earthquakes will strike. If they knew the places where earthquakes could cause the most damage, planners of cities could restrict those areas from development. Unfortunately, much of the world is already built up and continues to be developed with little regard to the possibility of earthquake danger. The best that can be done in many places is damage control—trying to find out where and when earthquakes will strike and do whatever is possible to minimize the damage.

Earthquake forecasting is an exciting branch of seismology and one that has had dramatic successes and deep disappointments. It requires a wealth of scientific information about the current condition of the earth. A wide array of instruments are put to the task, some even looking outward into space billions of light-years away for answers.

EARTHQUAKE INSTRUMENTATION

Like military commanders deploying their troops on the battlefield, seismologists deploy their instruments across the landscape to monitor earthquakes. Many instruments are employed to measure subtle long-term changes in the ground that could indicate an earthquake is coming.

Tiltmeters work like a carpenter's level (Figure 16). Two water-filled chambers are mounted on the earth's surface in an area suspected of having earthquake movements. Both chambers are connected with a tube. If the earth rises or tilts underneath one of the chambers, water runs out through the tube and raises the level in the lower chamber. You can experience the same thing with a water-filled garden hose. Raise one end and water gushes out the other. Lower one end and water rushes out of it. A measurement scale tells seismologists how much the ground tilted.

Gravimeters provide a measurement similar to tiltmeters (Figure 17). The device has a sensitive scale inside that can detect minute changes in gravity that take place when a mass of land is raised or lowered. Inside the gravimeter is a weight suspended so that if the force of gravity increases or decreases, the weight can move correspondingly. If rock rises up, the gravitational force is lessened a minute amount permitting the weight to rise slightly. If the rock lowers, the force

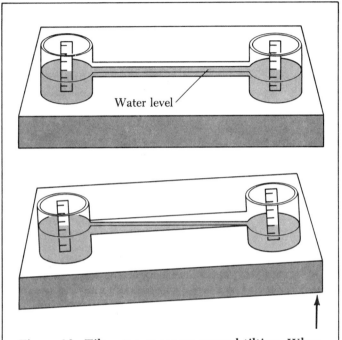

Figure 16. Tiltmeters measure ground tilting. When the earth rises or tilts, the water level in the lower chamber rises.

increases ever so slightly, pulling the inside weight down slightly. Very sensitive gravimeters can detect a change in elevation of only ½ inch (1 cm).

Strainmeters are placed in locations where seismologists suspect rock is spreading apart. The heart of a strainmeter is a long rod that is supported along its length so that it can rest freely without sagging. One end of the rod is anchored to the rock it is measuring

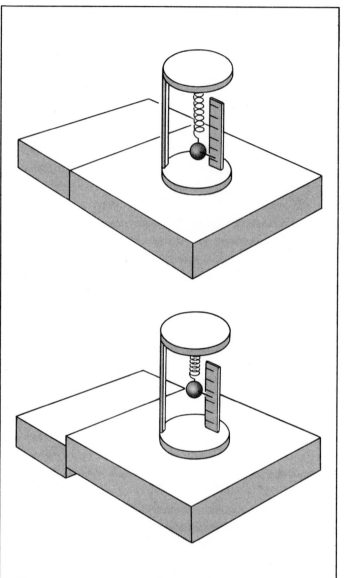

Figure 17. Gravimeters detect minute changes in gravity when a land mass is raised up or down.

and the other end remains unattached. A measuring scale is placed next to the free end of the rod. If the land pulls apart, even very slightly, the free end of the rod will have appeared to move. Actually the scale, mounted firmly to the rock below, is doing the moving. The rods for some strainmeters are hundreds of feet long.

Creepmeters are similar to strainmeters in that they measure changes in length of the earth's surface (Figure 18). The creepmeter is installed across a known fault line. Inside is a wire that is attached to a post anchored in the ground at one end and to a weight slung over a pulley at the other end. A pointer is attached to the weight and points to a measuring scale. If the two sides of the fault move in different directions, the weight rises or falls indicating a movement.

Magnetometers are sensitive devices that measure the direction of the earth's magnetic field. Strain in rock can alter the field very slightly. The detection of a change in the magnetic field can indicate pressure is building in rock, which could lead to an earthquake.

Laser range finders are useful for measuring slight movements between two points that are widely separated from each other (Figure 19). Two stations are mounted on opposite sides of a fault line. One station features a laser and an atomic clock. The other station has a reflector. A pulse of laser light is sent to the reflector station, which sends the pulse back to the sending station. The atomic clock is used to measure how long it took for the light pulse to travel to the reflector and back. Light travels at a velocity of 186,000 miles per second (300,000 km per second). Knowing that, it is a matter of simple arithmetic to determine exactly how far the two stations are from

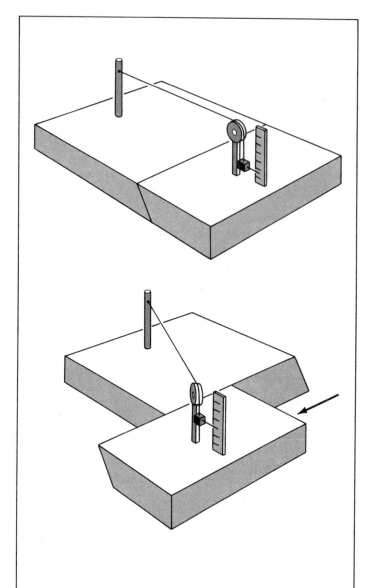

Figure 18. Creepmeters measure movement along a fault line.

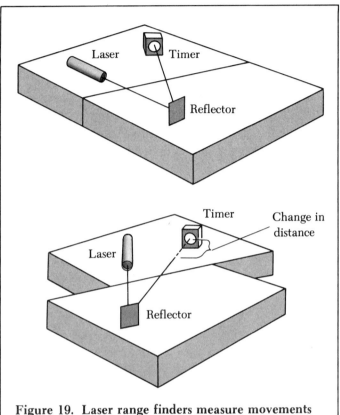

Figure 19. Laser range finders measure movements between two points by sending a pulse of laser light back and forth between a sending station and a receiving station.

each other. Weeks and months later additional measurements are made, and if any movement along the fault line has taken place to move the two stations nearer or farther apart than they were, the time it takes for the laser pulse to travel forth and back will be different. The difference in arrival times can be converted to a precise measurement of how far the land beneath has moved. Laser range finders are so accurate they can detect a change of only ⅕ inch over a distance of 10 miles (0.5 cm over 16 km).

An important variation of laser range finders is to use a distant reference point to reflect laser pulses. Light moves so rapidly that it is difficult to get a precise measurement when it travels forth and back over a short distance. A more accurate measure is possible when it travels a great distance before returning. One way to increase accuracy is to place the reference point in space. The NASA Laser Geodynamic Satellite (LAGEOS) is a space reference point orbiting high above the earth in a very well-known stable orbit (Figure 20). The satellite is a sphere, 24 inches (60 cm) in diameter, that looks like a giant golf ball. In each of the hundreds of dimples is a special reflector that bounces back laser beams in exactly the same direction from which they came. To take measurements, two laser stations send beams to the satellite and then measure the travel time of the reflected beams. If we know the satellite's orbit, its exact direction from the stations when the pulses were fired, and the travel time for the beams, we can determine the precise distance between the two stations. After several measurements are taken by the two stations over days or weeks, the amount of movement between the stations is calculated.

Still another variation of the laser range finders doesn't use lasers at all. Astronomical radio telescopes in widely separated locations look out into space at very distant quasars and radio galaxies. The arrival time of the radio waves from these objects at the radio telescopes is compared. If the land beneath the radio

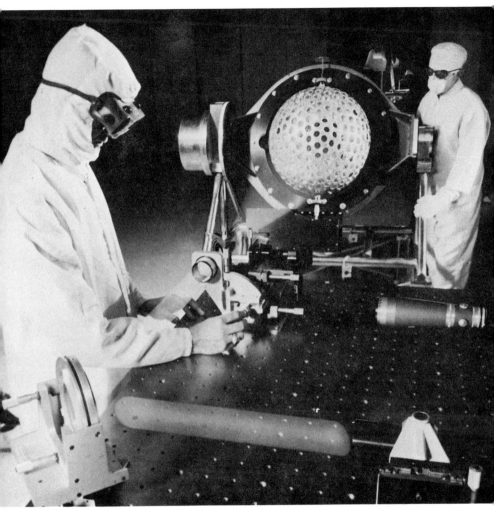

*Physicists test the LAGEOS satellite,
which provides a stable reference point in
the sky from which laser pulses are reflected
to their point of origin. By timing the
journey of the pulse, scientists can monitor
minute movements of the earth's crust.*

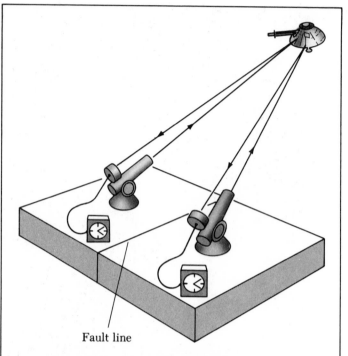

Fault line

Figure 20. The NASA Laser Geodynamic Satellite (LAGEOS) is used for laser distancing ranging to measure movement along a fault line. The great distance makes measurement more accurate than short-range laser pulses.

telescopes moves, the next time the radio waves are measured a time difference between the two stations will be revealed. Again, the time difference is used to calculate the distance of movement (Figure 21). This technique is especially useful for measuring movements of tectonic plates. Movement as slight as ½ inch (1 cm) per year is detectable.

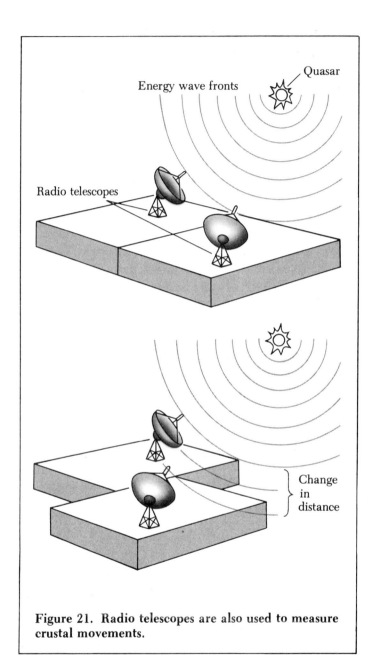

Figure 21. Radio telescopes are also used to measure crustal movements.

LAIONING PROVINCE, MANCHURIA, CHINA

Some of the most deadly earthquakes in history have struck China. Centuries of dense populations and many poorly built structures have made the Chinese especially susceptible to earthquake disaster. In the Laioning Province, people were especially wary. A number of small and moderate tremors had been plaguing the region. Water wells started bubbling, and mice and rats left their holes and began weaving about like drunks. Even snakes left their hibernation to lie frozen on icy roads. Local Communist party members began instructing people on what to do in the event of an earthquake.

On the morning of February 4, 1974, a swarm of tremors began and then suddenly became quiet. In the early afternoon, a military commander broadcast a radio message. "There probably will be a strong earthquake tonight. We require all people to leave their homes." As many as 3 million people put out their home fires and left to take shelter in straw structures and tents that had been set up in anticipation of a big earthquake. The people did not have to wait long. At 7:36, great sheets of light flashed through the sky. The ground heaved and buckled. Great jets of water and sand were squeezed out of the ground. Buildings fell. In the end, only 300 people died instead of the thousands that could have.

The Laioning prediction was a stunning success for the Chinese and in 1976 they tried again. This time the prediction was made for the Kwangtung Province. Residents were instructed to occupy temporary shelters. They remained there for two months but nothing happened. Concluding the prediction was mistaken, people were permitted to return until clearer signs of danger were detected. The clear signs never came and on July 28, 1976, an 8-magnitude earthquake struck Tangshan. The first earthquake was followed 16 hours later by a 7.4-magnitude earthquake. An additional 125 4-magnitude or above earthquakes struck in the following 16 hours. The region was a shambles.

Embarrassed by their failure to predict the Tangshan earthquake, the Chinese kept silent on the details of what had happened. It would be years before western scientists could piece together the magnitude of the horror. The number of people killed is still uncertain, but it is estimated to be in excess of 750,000. The Tangshan earthquake was the most deadly earthquake in over 400 years.

DILATANCY

On July 10, 1949, an earthquake hit the mountainous Garm region of Tadzhikistan in the south-central Soviet Union. When the shaking stopped, 12,000 people lay dead. This was not the first earthquake to strike the region. The previous October another earthquake 70 miles (113 km) to the west had killed 20,000 people.

The two earthquakes had a sobering effect on Soviet leaders and they became determined to do something about the situation. Scientists were dispatched to the region to try to find some way to protect the population. Careful observations of earth tremors passing through the area led to an important discovery. The Soviet scientists detected a drop in the velocity of body waves passing through the earth prior to the occurrence of an earthquake. Normally, P-waves travel about 1.77 times faster than S-waves.

However, prior to an earthquake striking, P-waves appeared to travel only 1.5 times faster than S-waves. The change in body-wave velocity only takes place within a few tens of miles of the coming earthquake, and therefore a large network of seismographs has to be set up to cover all points.

Another and equally important discovery is that the ratio of the P- and S-wave velocity returns to 1.77 a few hours or days before the earthquake strikes. To seismologists, this is almost as if the earth is "ringing a bell" telling them to watch out. Later scientific studies in other parts of the world pointed out that only the P-waves slow down and not the S-waves. This observation was important in explaining what was happening. Scientists now know a process called *dilatancy* is taking place.

Dilatancy is a change in the shape of mineral grains that make up rock when the rock is squeezed hard from opposite directions (Figure 22). Under pressure, the grains flatten out a bit and elongate themselves in a direction perpendicular to that pressure. The pressure comes from the buildup of the pushing forces that eventually are released with an earthquake. During this elongation, the grains also stretch out the pore spaces that exist between them. In other words, the rock has more openings in it than before. Normally, pores in rock are filled with water, but when the pores get bigger, they open up air spaces. This change has an important effect on the velocity of P-waves. P-waves are unaffected by water in the rock, but they do slow down traveling through air. The presence of more air in the rock slows P-wave velocity, accounting for the drop seen by Soviet scientists.

Pressure buildup on the rocks will continue for days, months, or years until the rock can no longer

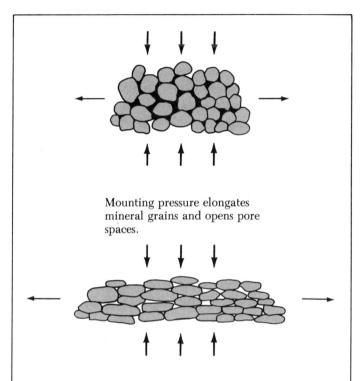

Mounting pressure elongates
mineral grains and opens pore
spaces.

Figure 22. Dilatancy is a change in shape of mineral
grains that takes place when rock is squeezed from
opposite directions. This change can be useful for
earthquake forecasting because P-waves move more
slowly through the air spaces opened up by dilatancy.

stand it and snaps in an earthquake. What happens
just before the breaking point is reached is very
important. Pressure has caused the mineral grains to
elongate and to create many new pore spaces filled
with air. The velocity of the P-wave drops. When the
mineral grains reach their limit and can elongate no

more without breaking, no new pore spaces are created. Ground water seeps into the pores to fill them, and this causes the velocity of P-waves to return to normal. This signals to seismologists that the earthquake is about to strike.

Measuring body-wave velocity has proven very successful in forecasting earthquakes on some but not all occasions. Seismologist Yash Aggarwal detected a drop in P-wave velocity in upper New York State in 1973. When the velocity returned to normal, he predicted an earthquake of a magnitude of about 2.5 would strike the area in a couple of days. Two days later, the earthquake struck.

Closely associated to body-wave velocity changes are changes in electrical conductivity of rock. The ground is able to pass a current of electricity. Two electrodes placed in the ground at opposite sides of an area of suspected future earthquake activity could indicate when an earthquake is likely to strike. When the pore spaces of rock are saturated with water, the conductivity of the rock is greater than when it has many open air spaces. Consequently, when dilatancy takes place the rock pores first expand, leaving many air gaps. Conductivity goes down. Near the last days before the earthquake strikes, the pores finally get refilled with water and conductivity goes up.

THE ARMENIAN DISASTER

On December 7, 1988, disaster struck another region of the Soviet Union, the Republic of Armenia. It was a normal Wednesday—children were studying in school, workers were busy in factories and offices, and people were shopping. The day began like any other but would not end that way. At 11:41 A.M. a shallow but strong earthquake of magnitude 6.9 struck. Its epicenter was 25 miles northeast of Leninakan, a city of 290,000. The earth shook for nearly a minute and by the time it stopped, whole cities were crushed. But the disaster was not complete. Four minutes later, a strong aftershock of magnitude 5.9 followed and lasted for nearly as long as the first quake.

The city of Spitak, where 30,000 people lived, was "erased from the face of the earth" according to a Soviet television commentator. Leninakan was nearly 80 percent destroyed. The clock tower in the city square remained standing with its clock hands frozen at 11:41. All buildings higher than two stories and within 30 miles (48 km) of the epicenter collapsed. Row upon row of nine-story apartment houses tumbled into dusty piles of rubble. Prefab concrete housing developments crumbled like "crackers." Elementary School No. 9 fell on the children within. Within days, rescue workers pulled out the bodies of 50 children. The destruction was extensive because of the poor construction of buildings throughout Armenia. Many structures, like the houses of the Armenian poor constructed of mud and rock, were unreinforced and simply shook apart.

As with most earthquake disasters, the earthquake itself was only the start of the nightmare. Fires ignited in many places and rescue and medical services were hampered by the great debris piles and the wandering of stunned and wailing survivors. There was a great shortage of heavy equipment to lift up the twisted debris and broken concrete slabs to get at people trapped beneath. Though eventually thousands were pulled out alive, many more may have perished because help arrived too late. Reports of the death toll rose rapidly by the tens of thousands as

officials tried to grasp the magnitude of the disaster. Varying totals reached upwards of 75,000 or more. Estimates were complicated by the great number of people left homeless (perhaps 500,000). It was difficult to know who was killed or trapped under the debris and who was wandering in shock.

The Soviet Union's new policy of *glasnost*, or openness, gave the world the opportunity to have an unprecedented look at the tragedy. A few years earlier, Soviet officials would simply not have made public a disaster of this scale. People around the world watched the tragedy on evening television newscasts. The result was a great outpouring of sympathy and offers of help. Specialized disaster rescue crews, including teams of dogs trained to sniff out survivors, descended on Armenia. Medical and other emergency supplies were shipped by the planeload. As with most disasters, the international rescue effort was hampered because the cities were in shambles and even movement across town was tedious. Yet the exhaustive effort paid off. More recent estimates place the human loss of the Armenian earthquake at around 25,000.

UNUSUAL HAPPENINGS

Testimony abounds regarding unusual happenings taking place just before an earthquake strikes. Many

A city in Soviet Armenia was reduced to rubble by a December 1988 earthquake. The clock is frozen at the time of the quake.

witnesses have reported that birds and other animals become restless hours before the ground begins trembling. In the city of Tianjin, China, zoo keepers reported that a tiger was depressed, yaks were not eating well, the pandas were screaming, swans kept out of the water, and the turtles were restless in the morning before an earthquake struck. Scientists believe there may be some validity to these observations. Many animals are more sensitive to their surroundings than humans, and vibration too faint to be detected by humans could agitate them. However, claims that some animals have been disturbed days before an earthquake are hard to prove because other factors, such as approaching severe weather, can have the same effect on animals and be misinterpreted as an earthquake warning.

Even stranger are changes that have been seen in ponds and irrigation canals by the Chinese. The ponds suddenly become muddy and give off unpleasant odors. Again, faint pre-earthquake ground tremors could stir up sediments and release gases from decaying organic matter in the sediment. Often in the moments prior to the earthquake striking the sky is set aglow with eerie neonlike flashes and balls of fire floating up from the ground. Scientists think methane gas is released from the ground, and it ignites through spontaneous combustion into glowing balls of fire. Flashes in the sky may be electric discharges lighting up gas—somewhat like the way an electric current passing through the gas contained within a fluorescent lamp tube causes gas atoms to give off light.

As forecasting aids for the seismologist, animal movements, flashes, and gas releases have limited value. For the most part, they take place just moments before the ground shakes. More important are observations, like P- and S-wave velocity changes, that take place days or months in advance. These kinds of observations give people time to prepare for the worst.

One such long-term observation was made by Japanese and Soviet seismologists who discovered that in some areas there can be tilting of the ground and a decrease in small earthquake activity prior to a big earthquake striking. Another pre-earthquake change has been detected in deep water wells. The water level in the well can suddenly change, perhaps in response to changes in ground pressure. An increase in the amount of radioactive radon gas dissolved in water may signal a change in pressure on the rock beneath the surface, forcing the gas into solution in the water. Each of these observations can be made some time in advance of an earthquake's arrival, alerting the seismologist to keep a closer eye on the region.

SEISMIC GAPS AND OTHER HISTORICAL EVIDENCE

In the early 1970s seismologist Lynn Sykes pointed out that in the belts of the earth that are most prone to earthquakes, some areas had not had an earthquake for a long time. It has long been known that the longer an earthquake-prone area goes without an earthquake the more likely one is coming soon. On the other hand, an area that has recently been hit is likely to be very quiet for some time. Sykes called the areas without recent activities *seismic gaps*. Further studies of the gaps have since indicated that they can be quiet for a very long time before small tremors begin. These small tremors provide a useful sign that a much bigger earthquake is due in a few days or weeks.

Historical studies of past earthquake activity, though not useful for precise forecasting of future earthquakes, can be helpful in determining trends in earth movements. One such survey of large earthquakes that have struck along the San Andreas fault near Wrightwood, California, has indicated the average time between large earthquakes there is 131 years. Researchers reached this conclusion by studying sediment layers in the region. The last large earthquake there was in 1857.

The area has already passed the 131-year average and another one is due. However, averages can be misleading. Saying the average time between earthquakes is 131 years means the next earthquake could take place anywhere from 50 years to 212 years hence. The area could be free from a future earthquake for many years even if the 131-year average has passed. But it is reasonable to conclude that as more time passes the chances increase that an earthquake will happen soon.

PUTTING IT
ALL TOGETHER

Seismologists now know much about earthquakes, and at times accurate forecasting of them seems to be nearly within their grasp. With an array of instruments studying the earth's interior, it is possible on occasion not only to say where and when but also how big. Unfortunately, forecasting techniques are not foolproof and mistakes are possible. Considering what a mistake could mean, seismologists are reluctant to make very specific forecasts. A wrong forecast could lead to widespread panic. How would people react if told their houses will fall down in the next hour? Should people be told to evacuate their cities? People in a hurry have accidents. A long-range forecast could greatly reduce property values and throw cities into economic depressions. Who would be responsible if a prediction was in error?

Regular earthquake forecasts are still some time off. First, seismologists have to improve their forecasting accuracy before taking the risk of telling people what may happen. After too many wrong forecasts, people will begin distrusting seismologists and not protect themselves. People also have to be educated as to what a forecast is. They have to learn that an earthquake forecast is like a weather forecast. A forecast is a probability statement. A 50 percent probability means that in 5 times out of 10 the earthquake will strike. It also means that in 5 times out of 10 it will not strike. The purpose of the forecast is to help people prepare for the worst.

CAN EARTHQUAKES BE CONTROLLED?

The important question arises of what to do about earthquakes. Can earthquakes be controlled? The U.S. Army's pumping of toxic water deep into the earth in the 1960s points to a possible control technique. Seismologists have suggested drilling three deep wells along a fault line that is building pressure for an earthquake. Water would be pumped out of wells 1 and 3, causing increased friction of the rock and locking the fault in those locations. Water would be pumped into well 2, lubricating the fault. The idea is to trigger a small earthquake between two locked

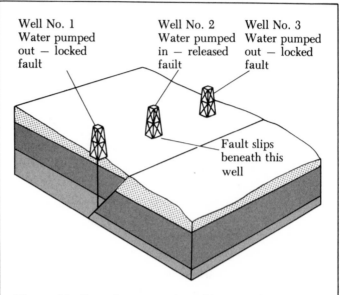

Well No. 1
Water pumped
out — locked
fault

Well No. 2
Water pumped
in — released
fault

Well No. 3
Water pumped
out — locked
fault

Fault slips
beneath this
well

Figure 23. Pumping water into the ground to gradually relieve the strain that might normally cause a strong earthquake is one proposed earthquake control technique.

areas so as to relieve some of the pressure (Figure 23). Next a fourth well is added to the line so that water is now pumped into well 3 and out of wells 2 and 4. Again a small earthquake is triggered, and a fifth well is added to the line. Eventually, the seismologists believe the strain of a major fault could be relieved and a major earthquake prevented. As promising as the technique seems, a major problem exists. Who pays for damage caused by the small earthquakes? Because it may take years to answer that question, the technique remains untried.

PREPARING
FOR EARTHQUAKES

How should people prepare for earthquakes? The first question is answered in a number of ways. Where you choose to live in earthquake-prone country is very important. If you live in houses built on soil bluffs like the houses in the Turnagain subdivision in Anchorage, Alaska, you are at great risk. Loose soil can greatly magnify the effects of the ground shaking and put you into grave danger. It is better to live on firm soil that is not subject to landslides carrying it away or to being covered by landslides coming down on it.

The safest kinds of houses to live in are wooden frame buildings that are tightly joined together and anchored to concrete foundations. Brick and stone buildings should be reinforced with steel. Especially dangerous are buildings with heavy tile roofs that can come shaking down on their interiors. Large buildings should be built to hold much greater weights than similar buildings built in areas not prone to earthquakes. Heavy ornamental concrete decorations should not be attached to the outsides of buildings. Many new building techniques exist that are designed to stand up under heavy earthquake conditions. Though plaster may crack and windows may break, these new techniques permit structures to survive all but the largest earthquakes. It is important for communities to have zoning laws that prohibit building in unsafe locations and putting up unsafe buildings.

What should people do when earthquakes strike? Even with properly constructed buildings built in the safest locations, you are still in danger if a major earthquake strikes. Most injuries and deaths do not come from ground movements but from being crushed by falling debris. Here are things you should—and should not—do if an earthquake strikes:

- Experts report that, usually, one of the worst things you could do is to run outside during an earthquake. Generally, more debris falls outside buildings than inside them, and many injuries and deaths are caused by falling debris outside.

- If indoors, remain there and get under a heavy table or a bed. Watch out for high bookcases and china cabinets. Stay away from windows, mirrors, and chimneys.

- If you are in a high-rise building, get under a desk. Stay out of stairways because they could become clogged with panicking people and may crack and come crashing down. Stay out of elevators because the power could be cut off, trapping you between floors.

- If you are outside, move away from high buildings, walls, power poles, and other tall objects that would fall on you.

Unfortunately, there are no rules that can protect you in all earthquake situations, but if you follow these suggestions you will greatly reduce your chances of being killed.

"A NOBLE EARTHQUAKE"

John Muir was a naturalist who lived much of his life in California. He loved nature and spent his life learning everything he could about it. One night, he experienced an earthquake. Muir later wrote about his feelings. "I ran out of my cabin, both glad and frightened, shouting. A noble earthquake! A noble earthquake!' feeling sure I was going to learn something." Earthquakes have indeed enabled scientists to learn about the earth's interior and have helped them explain how the continents came to be and why they look the way they do.

LIVING WITH EARTHQUAKES

Learning about earthquakes is an ongoing process. The more signs we identify that indicate when and where they are likely to strike, the more we will be able to do something about them. In time, it will be possible to forecast their arrival with a high degree of certainty. People will be able to move to relative safety and thousands of lives will be saved. A greater understanding of the motions and forces involved in earthquakes and how these affect structures will lead to the design of better buildings capable of surviving all but the largest earthquakes. Identifying areas of greatest earthquake hazard will permit forward-thinking land-use planners to restrict construction and encourage use of land for agriculture, parks, and natural areas. It may even become possible to release earthquake strain gradually before it reaches the breaking point and prevent the massive destruction entirely.

Earthquakes provide us with a challenge. We have learned that earthquakes are a force to be respected and feared, but we have also learned that earthquakes are neither good or evil. They exist as a part of the dynamic earth we live on. It is up to us to learn to live with them.

GLOSSARY

Aftershocks. Secondary earthquakes of a lesser magnitude that follow a much larger earthquake.

Amplitude. The sideways distance a seismograph needle moves as it records seismic waves.

Body waves. Seismic waves that travel through the earth.

Core. The innermost layer of the earth.

Creepmeter. A device that detects slow movements of rock on opposite sides of faults.

Crust. The outermost layer of the earth.

Dilatancy. The elongation of mineral grains and pore spaces in rock when the rock is squeezed.

Earthquake. Shaking of the earth caused by the sudden slippage of rock masses along a fault.

Elastic rebound. The springing back of deformed rocks to their original shapes during an earthquake.

Epicenter. The point on the surface of the earth directly above the focus of an earthquake.

Extensiometer. A detection device that can measure the movement of rock that is spreading apart.

Fault. A break in rock which is often accompanied by movement (earthquake) of rock masses on opposite sides of the break.

Fault line. The edge of a fault plane.

Fault plane. The surface between two masses of rocks that have been cut by a fault.

Focus. The place where movement along a fault plane begins, creating an earthquake.

Folds. Permanently bent rock layers.

Footwall. The underneath wall of a fault plane.

Foreshocks. Small tremors taking place prior to the main earthquake.

Gravimeter. A detection device that measures minute changes in gravitational force when rock layers are raised or lowered.

Hanging wall. The overhanging wall of a fault plane.

Inertia. The property all matter has that causes it to resist changes in motion.

Intensity. A measure of the surface effects of an earthquake.

Isoseismal lines. Map lines that circle areas of equal earthquake intensity.

Locked fault. Masses of rock that are kept from slipping along a fault plane by friction.

Love waves. Seismic waves that travel along the surface of the earth.

Low-velocity zone. A partially liquid layer within the earth that slows earthquakes from their theoretical speeds.

Magnetometer. A device that detects minute changes in the earth's magnetic field.

Magnitude. A measure of earthquake size.

Mantle. The middle layer of the earth's interior.

Microseisms. Very small continuous seismic waves.

Modified Mercalli Intensity Scale. A reference scale for determining the levels of earthquake intensity at the surface of the earth.

Normal fault. A fault in which the footwall moves up and the hanging wall moves down.

P-wave. The primary or fastest seismic body wave.

Plate tectonics. The theory that states the earth's crust is divided up into large plates that move with respect to each other, creating ocean basins, mountains, and earthquakes.

Pluton. A mass of hardened mantle rock that has thrust its way up partly into the crust.

Rayleigh waves. A surface seismic wave.

Reverse fault. A fault where the hanging wall moves up and the footwall moves down.

Richter scale. A scale for measuring the magnitude of an earthquake.

S-wave. The secondary or slower seismic body wave.

Seismic gaps. Areas in seismic-prone zones that have not been struck by an earthquake for a long time.

Seismic waves. Waves within and on the surface of the earth caused by earthquakes.

Seismograph. A recording device that measures the vibrations caused by earthquakes.

Seismologists. Scientists who study earthquakes and their effects.

Seismoscope. A device that senses earthquake vibrations but does not record them.

Strike. An imaginary horizontal line on the surface of tilted rock.

Strike-slip fault. A fault in which the motion is parallel to the strike line.

Subduction. The downward forcing of ocean floor plates by continental plates riding over them.

Surface waves. Seismic waves that travel at the earth's surface.

FOR FURTHER READING

Bolt, Bruce A. *Earthquakes*. New York: W. H. Freeman, 1988. (Advanced reading)

Bramwell, Martyn. *Volcanoes and Earthquakes*. New York: Franklin Watts, 1986. (Basic reading).

Gere, James M. and Haresh G. Shah. *Terra Non Firma— Understanding and Preparing for Earthquakes*. New York: W. H. Freeman, 1984. (Advanced reading)

Navarra, John Gabriel. *Earthquake*. Garden City: Doubleday & Company, Inc., 1980. (Basic reading)

Ritchie, David. *Superquake!* New York: Crown, 1988. (Advanced reading)

Simon, Seymour. *Danger from Below*. New York: Four Winds Press, 1979. (Basic reading)

Walker, Bryce. *Earthquake*. Alexandria: Time-Life Books, 1982. (Advanced reading)

INDEX

Page numbers in *italics* refer to illustrations.

Africa, 66
Aftershocks, 15, 33
Aggarwal, Yash, 88
Alaska, 11–15, *13*, 40
Animal movements, 92
Aristotle, 25
Armenia, 88–91, *90*
Army, U.S., 71, 95
Asia, 63, 64, 66–67
Atlantic Ocean, 63, 64–65, 66
Atwood, Robert B., 11–12

Babylonia, 25

Basalt, 65, 66
Benioff, Victor Hugo, 63–64
Bitumen, 25
Body waves, 35–36
  in earthquake forecasting, 85–88, 93
  focus location and, 51–55
  velocities of, 39, 51–53, 68–69, 85–88, 93
  See also P-waves; S-waves
Buildings, 38
  safety of, 97, 99

California, 19, 20, 40, 41, 94
Cemeteries, 50–51

Chang Heng, 44, 45, 46
Chenega Island, 40
China:
 earthquakes in, 18,
  84–85, 92
 seismoscope invented
  in, 44, 45, 46
Continental drift, 63–64, 68
Continents:
 mountainlike ridges
  mirroring outlines of,
  65
 plate tectonics and,
  65–68
Core, 69
Creepmeters, 77
Crescent City, Calif., 40, 41
Crust, 69, 71

Dilatancy, 85–88
 body-wave velocity and,
  85–88
 electrical conductivity
  and, 88

Earth:
 interior of, 43, 68–69
 magnetic field of, 77
 microseisms in, 50
Earthquake forecasting, 62,
 73–88, 91–95, 99
 body-wave velocity in,
  85–88, 93
 in China, 84–85
 dilatancy and, 85–88
 electrical conductivity
  of rock in, 88
 historical studies in, 94
 instruments in, 74–82

seismic gaps and, 93–
 94
social concerns in,
 94–95
unusual happenings in,
 91–93
Earthquake Lake, 31, 32
Earthquakes:
 absence of warning
  before, 23, 24
 controlling effects of,
  95–96
 danger of, 21
 detecting of, 44–46
 early theories about,
  24–25
 energy released in, 15,
  34–39, 43, 57–61
 as fact of life on earth,
  18–22
 frequency of, 18
 heaving motion during,
  34
 man-made, 71–72
 measuring of, 43–61
 non-plate tectonic,
  70–71
 places more likely to be
  subject to, 19–21,
  62–63, 93, 99
 preparing for, 97
 pressure leading to, 25,
  31–34, 67–68, 86–88,
  93
 probability of being
  killed or injured in,
  19
 roaring sound during,
  39

Earthquakes (*cont.*)
   sequence of events in,
     24
   unusual happenings
     before, 91–93
   what to do in, 97–98
Electrical conductivity, 88
Energy, 43, 57–61
   and intensity of effects,
     58–60
   magnitude of, 58, 60–61
   radiated as seismic
     waves, 34–39
   released in Good Friday
     Earthquake, 15
   source of, 67–68
Epicenters, 35
   plotted on map, 62–63
   surveys of region
     surrounding, 58–60
Europe, 66
Ewing, Maurice, 64–65

Fault lines, 28, 29, 31, 33
   controlled earthquakes
     along, 95–96
   detecting movement
     along, 77–80
Fault planes, 26, 28, 33
   energy released along,
     34
Faults, 28–30, 67
   locked, 33–34, 72,
     95–96
   movement at sides of,
     25–26, 28
   pressure and, 31–34
Fire balls, before
  earthquakes, 92

Fires, after earthquakes, 18,
  24, 25, 89
Flashes in sky, 92
Focus, 34
   depth of, 34, 63–64
   determining location of,
     36, 43, 50–57
Folds, 31
Footwalls, 28–30
Franklin, Benjamin, 25

Garm, 85
Gas releases, 92
Geological Survey, U.S., 56,
  58–59
God, 25
Gomorrah, 25
Good Friday Earthquake,
  11–15, *13*, 40
Gravimeters, 74–75
Greece, ancient, 25

Hanging walls, 28–30
Heat, 34, 66
Hebrews, ancient, 25
Hindu mythology, 24–25
Hoover Dam, 71, 72
Hurricanes, 23, 50

Indian Ocean, 65
Inertia, 44, 47, 48
Intensity, 58–60
Irrigation canals, 92
Isoseismal lines, 60

Kompkoff, Nicholas, 40
Kwangtung Province, 84–85

Laioning Province, 84

Landslides, 31, 97
Laser Geodynamic Satellite
   (LAGEOS), 80, *81*
Laser range finders, 77–82
   on opposite sides of
      fault lines, 77–80
   with reference point in
      space, 80–82, *81*
Lisbon, 15–18, *16*
Locked faults, 33–34, 72
   triggering earthquakes
      between, 95–96
Logarithmic scales, 61
Love, A. E. H., 37
Love waves, 35, 37–38
Low-velocity zone, 69

Madison River, 31
Magnetometers, 77
Magnitude, 58, 60–61
Mantle, 69, 71
Mathematics, 37, 51–57
Mead, Lake, 71, 72
Mercalli, Giuseppe, 58
Methane, 92
Microseisms, 50
Mid Atlantic Ridge, 65, 66
Mineral deposits, 28
Mississippi River, 19, 31
Modified Mercalli Intensity
   Scale, 58–60
Moho Discontinuity, 69
Mohorovičić, Andrija, 69
Molten rock, 71
Mountains:
   folded rock in, 31
   formation of, 21–22, 30,
      67
   in ocean ridges, 65, 66

Muir, John, 98–99

NASA, 80
National Earthquake
   Information Center
   (NEIC), 55–57, *56*
Neumann, Frank, 58
New Madrid, Mo., 19, 71
New York State, 88
Normal faults, 26, 28–29, 30
North America, 66

Ocean floor, 18
   concentration of
      earthquakes on,
      62–65
   Ewing's study of, 64–65
   rock on, 65
   subduction on, 63–64,
      66–67
   tsunamis and, 42

Pacific Ocean:
   concentration of
      earthquakes in, 62,
      63–64
   mountain ridge in, 65
   subduction in, 63–64,
      66–67
Pendulums, 44, 45, 46–47,
   48
Plate tectonics, 21–22,
   65–68
   measuring of, 82
   pressures built through,
      67–68
   subduction and, 66–67
Pluton, 71
Ponds, 92

Poseidon, 25
Pressure, 25, 93
    controlled earthquakes
        and, 95–96
    detecting buildups of,
        77
    dilatancy and, 85–88
    faulting caused by,
        31–34
    plate tectonics and,
        67–68
    released at focus, 34
    rocks bent under, 31
Prince William Sound, 14,
    40
P-waves, 35
    distance to earthquake
        focus calculated from,
        36, 51–53, 55
    in earthquake
        forecasting, 85–88, 93
    roaring sound due to,
        39
    in study of earth's
        interior, 69
    velocity of, 35, 51–53,
        55, 68, 69, 85–88, 93

Radio telescopes, 80–82
Radon gas, 93
Rayleigh, Lord, 35
Rayleigh waves, 35, 38
Reverse faults, 26, 29, 30
Richter, Charles F., 60–61
Richter scale, 60–61
Rift valleys, 31
Rock:
    dilatancy in, 85–88
    elastic nature of, 31–33

    electrical conductivity
        of, 88
    on ocean floor, 65
    sedimentary, 26, 28, 30
    volcanic basalt, 65, 66
Rocky Mountain Arsenal, 71

San Andreas fault, 20, 94
Satellites, 80, 81
Sedimentary rock, 26, 28,
    30
Seismic gaps, 93–94
Seismic waves, 24, 34–39,
    65
    body vs. surface, 35
    Love, 35, 37–38
    measuring of, 43–50
    Rayleigh, 35, 38
    spherical movement of,
        34
    in study of earth's
        interior, 43, 68–69
    velocities of, 39, 51–53,
        55, 68–69
    vertical, 48–49
    See also Body waves;
        P-waves; Surface
        waves; S-waves
Seismographs, 46–50, 86
    amplitude of zigzags in
        records of, 61
    arrival-time differences
        recorded by, 51–53
    comparing of records
        from, 53–55
    and direction of
        earthquake waves, 48
    linked in worldwide
        network, 55

Seismic waves (*cont.*)
  to measure vertical
    waves, 48–50
  recording devices in,
    47, 48
Seismometers, 43–46, *45*
  in seismographs, 46–47,
    48
Seismoscopes, 44
Sky events, 92
Sodom, 25
Soil, loose vs. firm, 97
South America, 63–64, 66
Soviet Union, 85, 88–91, *90*
Standardized Seismograph
  Network, 55
Strainmeters, 75–77
Strikes, 30
Strike-slip faults, 26, 30
Subduction, 63–64, 66–67
Surface waves, 35, 36–38
S-waves, 35–36
  distance to earthquake
    focus calculated from,
    36, 51–53, 55
  in earthquake
    forecasting, 85–86, 93
  in study of earth's
    interior, 69
  transmitted through
    solid materials only,
    39, 68

velocity of, 36, 51–53,
  55–56, 85–86, 93
Sykes, Lynn, 93

Tadzhikistan, 85
Tangshan, 85
Tectonic plates. *See* Plate
  tectonics
Telescopes, radio, 80–82
Tianjin, 92
Tiltmeters, 74
Tombstones, 50–51
Tornadoes, 23
Toxic waste, 71, 95
Tsunamis, 14–15, 24, 40–42,
  41

Valleys, 30–31
Vema, 64–65
Volcanoes, 23, 62, 67, 71

Wadati, Kiyoo, 63
Water wells, 93
Waves. *See* Seismic waves;
  Tsunamis
Wegener, Alfred, 63, 64, 68
Wood, Harry, 58

Yellowstone National Park,
  31, 32

Zoning laws, 97